Starfish Detectives

Starfish Detectives

Sirens in a Changing Sea

Marie De Santis

ISBN: 1981713115
ISBN 13: 9781981713110

Contents

Healthy ochre sea star, *(photo, Claudia Rodman)*

1

Distant Early Warning
–Dr. Steve Fradkin

Dr. Steve Fradkin, Olympic National Park, (*photo, National Park Service*)

ERE YOU HAVE a true suspense filled tale of marine scientists caught unexpectedly on the crisis edge of an environmental catastrophe.

In June 2013, ecologist Steve Fradkin began alerting colleagues to the startling observations he was making out on the remote Pacific shores of Washington's Olympic National Park. The starfish that for eons had flourished on this rocky northwest coast were overnight turning into mushy globs of goo. As unsettling as the news was, it didn't begin to prepare these veteran marine scientists for the ghastly reports that would soon start pouring in from marine stations up and down the Pacific coast from Alaska all the way into Mexico.

The iconic sea stars were eroding limbs and melting away by the millions, often from one day to the next, in one locale after another, on the full length of the coast. It was fast becoming the largest marine wildlife disease ever recorded.

The blistering speed of the demise and its unprecedented scope would be alarming enough in any species. But the most afflicted starfish were also the keystone species and top predators of our prolific ocean shores. Beyond not knowing the cause of the disaster, no one had any idea how this astronomic loss would affect the huge constellation of marine species that thrive in the starfish's domain.

It was only a generation ago that marine scientists were regarded as the free-wheeling outliers of the scientific world, whiling away their time splashing around in tide pools. It didn't help the impression that most of their laboratories and classrooms have been set in remote coastal outposts far from the main academic centers.

Over the last few decades, however, these same marine scientists have begun finding themselves increasingly on the hot seat in the planet's most pressing scientific debates. The starfish demise, with its fever pitched search for answers and unparalleled attention from the press, thrust these scientists even more into the media's glare, calling on them to navigate an anxious public through the tempests of global warming, species extinctions, ocean acidification, Fukushima radiation, pandemic diseases, and more.

Starfish Detectives, Sirens in a Changing Sea is the heroic story of how, without protocols, infrastructure, nor funds earmarked for such events, these scientists rallied to the occasion volunteering weekends, nights, and months to ferret out the disaster's causes and consequences. It's also an enlightening account of how they dramatically advanced our understanding of life in the sea and its vital connections to all of us.

Ochre star in the throes of disease, *(Photo, Melissa Miner)*

2

Just Pure Good Luck
–Dr. Peter Raimondi
Chair, Department of Ecology, UC Santa Cruz

Dr. Peter Raimondi *(photo, Melissa Miner)*

IN EARLY SUMMER 2013, as word spread among scientists of the catastrophic scale of the starfish die-off, there wasn't a dime earmarked to deal with such events. There was no Center for Disease Control to take charge, no protocols or infrastructure to guide first steps, nor any lineup of first responders. Many of those who would soon be working most closely and intensely on the sea star disaster had never even met.

Nonetheless, for the diverse array of scientists being drawn into the vortex of events, there were some amazing strokes of luck and some fortuitous banks of data to light their way. Dr. Peter Raimondi and the work of his team at UC Santa Cruz were both.

For two decades starting in the early 1990s Raimondi and his team had been undertaking a methodical painstaking census of the Pacific coast's rocky intertidal life. Year after year, rain, fog, or biting wind, they returned to the same selected sites along the coast, laid out their transect tapes and squares over the exact same rocks, and lined them up along the precise coordinates where they had been the year before. At each visit, using identical methods, they would count and catalogue the countable critters, such as starfish, crabs, limpets, and snails. And with flora, such as marine algae and grasses, they would log the percentage of physical area covered. Year after year, the data were gathered, amassed, archived, and analyzed.

The primary funder of this massive data gathering was the National Bureau of Ocean Energy Management.

The main goal of the funding was to establish a biological baseline that could be referred to in cases of oil spills or other untoward events. By 2013, not surprisingly given the magnitude and duration of the project, there was also a crescendo of grumbling about whether the huge amounts of money needed to sustain the effort was worth it, especially given that the array of species being monitored had virtually no commercial clout.

There wasn't a hint that Raimondi and his work were about to become grand central station in a scramble for answers to a wildlife catastrophe that continues undiminished to this day. As monumental a task as Raimondi's work was up to this point, its value seemed to fit a natural academic progression in the unsung marine biology that preceded it. Unsung, that is, but for a singular legendary character who was lifted to fame by way of his fictional portrayal in John Steinbeck's 1945 classic, Cannery Row.

In the 1940s Cannery Row in Monterey, California was the bustling hub of a bonanza sardine fishery. It was a maritime gold rush of sorts, complete with a dockside melee of marginal characters who revolved around it. Steinbeck drew these characters into his novel with all their color; He set his main character 'Doc' in the midst of their motley tribes. A lone intellectual, a disciplined collector of tide pool organisms, and the waterfront's scientist and librarian, Doc was Steinbeck's barely fictionalized rendering of the real life Monterey tide pool explorer Ed Ricketts.

In flesh as in fiction Ricketts did more than his share to give the field of marine biology its free-wheeling, outlier reputation, populated by scientists unconcerned with academic fame. By day, he single-mindedly observed, collected and catalogued the astonishingly rich array of the shore's intertidal life. By night, he cavorted and philosophized with the roving bands of dock folk who frequented his makeshift waterfront lab. Buoyed by the novel's broad popularity his infatuation with the area's spectacular marine life was engraved in the public's mind.

An astute naturalist and consummate writer, Ricketts also gave marine science one of its touchstone texts. First published in 1939, the book's encyclopedic scope was matched by its behemoth original title, "Between Pacific Tides, An Account of the Habits and Habitats of Some Five Hundred of the Common, Conspicuous Seashore Invertebrates of the Pacific Coast Between Sitka, Alaska, and Northern Mexico". Revised editions of this hefty reference are still being published today under the more palatable title of "Between Pacific Tides", and it's still to be found within arm's reach of present day marine scientists and beach combers alike.

In the late 1980s as an undergraduate biology student at the desert-bound Northern Arizona University, Raimondi's nascent career hardly seemed on a trajectory to make a quantum leap off Rickett's work. But as luck would have it, for a brief time coinciding with Raimondi's enrollment, the Arizona university maintained a marine field station on Mexico's Sea of Cortez just south of the state's border.

In another turn of fate, Raimondi was engaged in studies at the field station right at the time a sea star die-off took place in the area's Mexican waters. It was an epidemic, says Raimondi looking back, whose cause was never determined in a population of stars that has ominously never recovered. But that confluence of events did ignite Raimondi's impassioned marine career.

Subsequently, while working on his doctoral degree in marine biology at UC Santa Barbara, Raimondi was introduced to the rigors of his chosen work monitoring intertidal areas. From the start he viewed the work as much more than a rote and repetitive cataloguing of tidal life. Influenced by the burgeoning concepts of ecology, he understood that the data sets he was gathering were elaborate dynamic renderings of bio-communities that could yield a wealth of insights into ecology's central questions about how marine organisms interact and interdepend.

These same emerging ecological concepts seemed to be shaping the innovative ways Raimondi and his colleagues set out to work together. Early on in 1991, far ahead of its time in terms of scientific collaboration, Raimondi and his colleagues had created a uniquely functioning pan coastal network. They called it MARINe, an acronym for the Multi Agency Rocky Intertidal Network.

On the one hand MARINe was loosely structured. It had no funding of its own. Individual participants like

Raimondi had funding for their own projects, but no one received a salary for participating in the MARINe network. Additionally, any team interested in carrying out the intertidal monitoring work could join.

On the other hand, MARINe operated according to a set of very strict rules. On joining, participants had to agree to adhere to all the same protocols in monitoring a given site and for sharing data. They also had to agree to meet at least once a year.

But most remarkable and groundbreaking was that despite its lack of funding and its focus on organisms of little academic prestige, the MARINe network quickly began attracting eager participation from an astonishing diversity of teams. There were teams joining from academia and government, from state and national parks, from native tribes, and from aquariums and zoos, from California, Oregon, Washington, British Columbia, and Alaska.

By the summer of 2013, MARINe participants had been voluntarily operating together for over 20 years with the kind of interdisciplinary collaboration that today is the envied but elusive goal of many other scientific endeavors. Cancer researchers, for example, have all agreed for some time that scientists absolutely must find a way to break out of their isolated silos of expertise to start sharing data and collaborating across disciplines. But they've too often failed to overcome the entrenched barriers of jealousies, orthodoxy, and bunkered turfs.

Perhaps it was the very outsider status of marine science that stoked MARINe's phenomenal inter-agency collaboration, providing, as it did, a welcoming collegial refuge from academia's neglect. In any case, there's no doubt that MARINe's unique collaboration was producing extraordinary results. By the summer of 2013 Raimondi and his partners were regularly monitoring over 150 intertidal sites from Alaska to Mexico, all using consistent agreed on methods.

"When the sea star wasting syndrome first came along," says Raimondi, "the program we had already up and running incorporated answering exactly the questions we wanted to answer for this disease, including monitoring where the disease was, the rate at which it was spreading, how virulent it was, the effects on the rest of the community, and recovery dynamics. We were already looking at those parameters!"

In a typical understatement of just how critical MARINe data would become as the disaster ravaged ever more territory raising ever more alarm, Raimondi says, "It was just pure good luck!"

"We did a little bit of additional work," he says, "but for the most part we kept doing what we had been doing because that (census) information was so valuable to the other investigators who wanted to follow the disease." "It really was good luck," he added. "If this outbreak had happened any other place, in fact it is happening on the east coast,.." and Raimondi's voice trails off.

MARINe's deep bank of data had another benefit for the epidemic response. It was a magnetic draw to researchers from disparate fields and far flung places to jump in and address the myriad pressing questions surrounding the sea star event.

Raimondi's enormous data on intertidal communities along the affected areas and his existing network of colleagues promised newcomers a solid platform of knowledge from which to launch their own inquiries. Two investigators in particular who jumped in from landlocked Cornell University in upstate New York, Dr. Ian Hewson and Dr. Drew Harvell, would soon prove to be key in identifying the epidemic's likely pathogen.

There was something else that would put Raimondi and his team in the center of the urgent efforts to understand this unprecedented disease. Most research teams have a report writer to chronicle their work. But Raimondi had years ago concluded that report writing was too slow a process that ended with a paper report that ended up in a drawer. Raimondi wanted something more immediate, more interactive, and more available to other researchers. Instead of a report writer for his scientific team, he hired a web designer.

More than anything else Raimondi credits the MARINe website for making his lab the cyber base camp for investigators near and far in their response to the sea star disease. The website was already designed to handle exactly the kind of real-time data input, interactive maps, summations, and inter-agency coordination that would be needed for the herculean job ahead. All the bugs had already been worked out. The website at seastarwasting. org and Raimondi's work continue as the hub today.

There was one thing, however, that no one on Raimondi's team or any of the others was prepared for, or had ever experienced, or even in their wildest imaginations could have anticipated.

During Raimondi's two plus decades of research, he recalls a grand total of perhaps 20 inquiries from the press. When the sea star wasting disease hit, he says, he was getting that many press calls a day. "We had film crews coming up. They were embedded with us. It was like a war zone in a lot of ways," he says. "They were competing with each other to be out in the field with us, and out on the boats with us. There were lots of times I was afraid someone was going to get killed."

'Journalist overboard' wasn't the only risk Raimondi faced in the media storm, as he was soon to learn the hard way. In the Fall of 2013, press coverage of the starfish die-off was at a peak right alongside horror-movie-like headlines reporting islands of radiated Fukushima trash closing in on the American West coast.

The broad array of scientists involved with the die-off, including Raimondi, had early on concluded that the Fukushima radiation had nothing to do with the sea star mortality. Most significantly, the specific isotopes of Fukushima concern were being closely monitored all along the coast and had never gone above background level at the time starfish became diseased, virtually eliminating that radiation as a cause.

But given the repeated coupling in time and headlines of the two startling ocean stories, the public was not to be so easily convinced. Indeed, even now years later the very first question scientists still often get from reporters regarding sea star disease is, "Could Fukushima radiation be the cause?"

Back in December 2013, when a reporter asked Raimondi this Fukushima question, Raimondi thought he was answering with the proper caution called for at the beginning of any investigation. "We're not throwing anything out yet," he told the reporter. The next morning, Raimondi was aghast when the San Francisco Chronicle published his quote under the headline, "Fukushima Radiation Possible Culprit in Huge Starfish Die Off from Alaska to Mexico." It was like gasoline being poured on the media fire.

But, he adds, "I was surprised. For the most part the media was pretty responsible, much more so than I had expected." And what was truly more "pure good luck" for the public is that Raimondi, like many of the sea star scientists tossed unexpectedly into the deep end of a media maelstrom, they seemed to have a flare for it.

Like most scientists they took great care not to overstate results. They also took particular care not to step on each other's expertise. "When the press wanted to talk about 'communities'" says Raimondi, "I was happy to talk communities. When they wanted to talk about 'viruses' I referred them to Ian."

Unlike many scientists in other fields, the marine biologists working on the sea star disease embraced their unique opportunity to communicate with the public. They took to it, you might say, like ducks to water.

3

People Were Calling Us in Tears
--Melissa Miner, MS

Research Associate, UC Santa Cruz,
Western Washington University

(*photo, David Lohse*)

Melissa Miner
(*photo, Ben Miner*)

ONE COULD SAY it started about a century ago with the cuddly teddy bear inspired by Teddy Roosevelt's fabled refusal to shoot a trapped bear. The decades since have delivered a succession of winsome animals coaxing humanity to better our bonds with all animals. From dolphins, pandas, and seal pups, right up to Cecil the lion, these compelling wildlife ambassadors opened a softer spot in human hearts.

Somehow, inexplicably among them, is the mute, mindless, and seemingly motionless starfish. By any measure the starfish is the antithesis of cuddly. It doesn't roll over, suckle furry young, or blink with soulful eyes, and it's an economic no-show to boot. Yet, the starfish is unquestionably a star! A seashore ambassador par excellence!

There isn't a kindergarten kid in Nebraska who can't call out its name and draw its radiant form with starry-eyed delight. Nor is starfish charisma limited solely to juvenile glee. Check any display of greeting cards and you're sure to see artistic renditions of beloved starfish helping convey every human emotion from love to condolence, to courage and carefree days.

Of all the things about the looming sea star disaster that has astonished even the most reserved scientists, the public's overwhelming emotional reaction was perhaps most mystifying of all.

"People were calling us in tears," exclaims marine biologist Melissa Miner! "It's been a signature of this event that people have this huge emotional attachment to the starfish," she says. "It's still a surprise to us today, this huge public reaction!"

"We'd been through another disease," says Miner, "the black abalone disease in Southern California. The black abalone was an economically important species. It was a prized gastronomic delicacy as well. It was upsetting to see hundreds and hundreds of animals disappear," she says, "but it was an interesting contrast how little interest there was in the black abalone die off."

Whatever the reason behind this extraordinary public outpouring of emotion for the starfish, the MARINe scientists, Miner among them, immediately recognized its stellar potential. For many years MARINe partners had been trying to figure out how to incorporate citizen science into their work. But they had never been able to find a way to mesh nonprofessional participation with the precision required to rigorously monitor intertidal sites.

The starfish wasting disease, however, quickly struck the team as an obvious citizen science match. The sea stars themselves were highly recognizable, especially the most common showy orange and purple ochre stars that live in accessible intertidal areas. From Alaska into Mexico, it's these plump colorful stars, speckled with patterned white dots, that parents excitedly point to and delighted kids dash into tide pools to touch. Of the 20 or more species of sea stars afflicted by the disease, the ochre star species was also one of the two hardest hit.

Another plus for the citizen science possibility was that the disease itself was so shockingly unmistakable. The jagged white lesions consuming the starfish arms are fulminating and grotesque. The necrotizing arms become gooey and are deeply disturbing to those who view it. "Once you see it," says Miner, "there's not much likelihood of mistaking it."

But it was the crucial data that citizens could provide that made organizing a citizen science effort an utmost priority. There was no way that the scientists by themselves could do the critical fine-tuned mapping of the disease over the thousands of miles of the affected coasts.

Mapping disease spread as early as possible, in as much detail as possible, is the first order of business in any epidemiological quest, whether the disease occurs on land, at sea, in humans or starfish. Real time mapping provides priceless clues as to possible primary and secondary causes, the mode of transmission, the factors affecting virulence and lethality, and the correlating vulnerabilities such as age, species, and habitat.

And time is of the essence. If disease spread isn't mapped as it occurs it's usually impossible to go back at a later date when all the starfish are gone to recreate the pathways of destruction.

There was a final impetus for going full speed ahead with a citizen science response. With just a few tweaks

Pete Raimondi's existing MARINe website would make it a cinch for people to input their observations of sea star status on their favorite hometown beaches.

The sea star citizen science program was given a unanimous go. Melissa Miner, a charter member of the MARINe network, was put in charge. Her life, like that of virtually every other scientist who stepped into the fray, was instantly consumed by the blitz of the disease. Overnight, her days and weeks became a far cry from the sunny sandy summers that first sparked her love of all things marine.

Miner's family had spent their summers in Santa Cruz. It was there in long carefree days at the beach that young Melissa became mesmerized by the critters she found and played with. When a high school science teacher gave her the idea that she could make a career of it the die was cast.

Following a BS at UC Santa Cruz, and MS from the UC Moss Landing Marine Lab, Miner headed back to Santa Cruz to work with Pete Raimondi right in time to join in the early days of MARINe.

Despite her own extensive experience in intertidal monitoring, being put in charge of the citizen science program set her world spinning around a whole new set of requirements for the job. As she herself says, "I developed it on the fly."

The first obvious step was to adapt the MARINe protocols so they were accessible for public use. These new protocols, along with sea star identification keys, interactive data maps, data input guides, and news updates, all needed to be incorporated into an offshoot of the MARINe website. The new website, seastarwasting.org, was launched.

"We also adapted for habitats that MARINe didn't normally work in," says Miner. "For example, pier pilings have been a great place where people could do repeat observations."

Another key task for Miner was finding and training groups that had previous citizen science experience, groups that would be there for the long haul. Miner trained and worked with local dive clubs that volunteered for some of the underwater work. Natural history and conservation groups were recruited and trained for long-term monitoring of the disease in intertidal areas. "I was spending a lot of time traveling around trying to balance everything with two young children. It was tricky."

Miner's work was made even trickier by the fact that even as she feverishly worked to get the program up and running, a blizzard of unsolicited observations was pouring in helter-skelter from beach goers up and down the coast. These were people who happened on the diseased starfish and were horrified by what they were seeing. One way or another they were finding their way to marine scientists to express their alarm, and the marine scientists, in turn, were funneling them all over to Miner.

Despite not having any pre-training, the observations from every one of these impromptu citizen scientists were vital to understanding the disease's spread. But their data needed special vetting. So in addition to her other jumble of tasks, Miner had to set up a system to evaluate all the information coming in, as it were, over the transom. "In cases where we didn't know the people, for example, we'd ask them to go back and take some photos to make sure the observations were credible."

Tracking the devastation only intensified over the year as the sea star disease, very uncharacteristically in wildlife diseases, alarmingly jumped to over 20 species and radiated out from nodal points from Alaska to Mexico. The vast underwater fields of bleak carnage in the wake of the disease left scientists intoning their shock with words like "unprecedented", "catastrophic", "uncharted territory", "the largest marine wildlife disease ever recorded".

The acknowledgements at the bottom of the disease data page at http://data.piscoweb.org/marine1/seastardisease.html lists the names of over 600 individuals who contributed data to the original mapping of disease incidents. The overwhelming number of those names are the individual citizen scientists who pitched in whole heartedly to help.

Because of this public participation, scientists now had vital information that went beyond just the scope and spread of the disease. Intriguing details were beginning to emerge out of the data. Though their significance wasn't yet understood, these details would become highly useful in ruling in or ruling out various hypotheses about what was causing such devastation.

The data was revealing the relative disease vulnerabilities among the sea star species, and that the sunflower and ochre star were the most afflicted. The data was also showing that younger starfish for whatever reason were much less susceptible to the disease than the adults, that higher water temperatures seemed to increase the virulence, and that aquariums that pumped in ocean sea water, even those that used filters, lost all their starfish to the disease.

Up until the sea star wasting event, citizen science, with a few notable exceptions, had mostly been viewed as a way to engage and educate the public in science through active involvement. The public's massive role in mapping the sea star wasting disease greatly expanded that perception. It made the sea star program a showcase for the potential and power of citizen science to truly contribute to the science as well as to learn from it.

As much as this extraordinary public response to the sea star disease was a signature and legacy of the event's first year, so too was the unprecedented reaction of the scientists themselves.

Citizen scientists Bert and Gery,
(photo, Fiero Marine Life Center)

For all her weeks and months setting up and running the citizen science program Melissa Miner didn't receive one cent of pay. Like most of the scientists drawn to the sea star investigation, Miner made an initial effort looking high and low for emergency funds earmarked for such events. After applying to a score of possibilities, and being rejected or getting no response at all, Miner did what virtually every other involved investigator would do. She simply gave up looking for money and got to work.

Miner, in fact, was luckier than most. Though she never got funds to pay for her time, she was one of only two or three scientists who were at least able to get some quick funds to pay some of her expenses. Oregon Sea Grant gave the citizen science program $10,000 to pay for materials and travel. But her time, her work, and her expertise, were all volunteered.

The lack of emergency funds was exasperating. "At the same time," says Miner, "the work was exciting...I had not experienced anything like this before, never, never, anything like this. It did feel a little overwhelming, but that's why we're doing this kind of monitoring precisely for events like this – or for oil spills, or big disease events, things that are having a big impact on intertidal zones"

"It was a new thing we hadn't seen before. And it was exciting to have people interested in our work."

While the sea star event showed the enormous potential of citizen science, it was also about to underscore its limitations.

After the epidemic's first year, the task of mapping disease range and spread was winding down. Investigatory priorities shifted to more difficult questions. These included questions about the nature of the disease, determining the pathogen, working out the genomics, and defining the roles of physical environmental factors, such as ocean temperature, hypoxia, and ocean acidity. "Just operating the temperamental instrumentation to get an ocean pH reading," says Miner, "takes a level of expertise and precision that doesn't lend itself to citizen science."

Even looking for and mapping possible signs of recovery proved beyond the abilities of most citizen scientists. Miner put the graphics and annotations needed to identify baby sea stars of different species and placed it all on the web site. But the difficulties citizen scientists had using the information were soon evident.

Baby sea stars are only a few millimeters in size, making them difficult to find in the first place. Even if found their tiny size makes it especially difficult to differentiate one species from another.

Miner is thrilled to have had the practical contact with citizen science. "It's been a valuable experience for me." The program opened up a whole new facet of science not just to Miner but to all the other scientists who benefited from the extraordinary information base created through the public's participation. "I've been able to give back to the community in ways I couldn't before. It's definitely been a positive experience."

4

No Smoking Gun
–Dr. Martin Haulena, DVM
Chief of Veterinary Medicine, Vancouver Aquarium

Dr. Martin Haulena *(photo, Vancouver Aquarium)*

IN THE FALL of 2013, as devastating outbreaks of the sea star disease continued to flare up along the coast, the stars residing in many of the West Coast's premier aquariums were succumbing as well. Significantly, sea stars in the aquariums that drew water from the sea were afflicted – but not the stars in aquariums that made their own sea water.

Along with the observed patterns of disease spread, this fact supported growing speculation that the causative agent was a waterborne pathogen or toxin. Clearly, however, this didn't narrow things down to the point where anyone was even close to identifying a culprit. There were still as many theories being batted around about the causes of the epidemic as there were new reports of dead and dying starfish.

Some conjectured that the die-offs might even be a completely natural consequence of the overpopulation of some sea star species that had been observed in recent years.

The waters of the Salish Sea, for example, which includes Puget Sound and the inside sea of British Colombia, had seen a notorious and widespread overpopulation of the sunflower star. This spectacular star, with its uniquely dazzling array of 16 to 24 arms, in as many colors, is the largest, fastest, and most predatory of the West Coast stars. Leading up to the epidemic, the big concern wasn't for the sunflower star. It was for the myriad other sea floor invertebrates this ravenous predator was devouring in its path.

Now, oddly, it was the sunflower star of the 20 or more species afflicted by disease that was observed suffering the highest mortality rates. In many underwater fields where one week divers saw sunflower stars literally carpeting the sea floor, in the same spot a week later not one could be found. In many locales, lethality rates for the sunflower stars were an alarming 100%.

Another suspect in the epidemic was a protozoa infestation implicated in earlier smaller sea star die-offs. Still another theory posited a pollutant trigger. This was based on the proximity of many of the die-off hotspots to metropolitan areas, while the more sparsely populated Oregon coast, at the time, was relatively unscathed. A sister theory was that ocean warming was the trigger, since Oregon waters that summer were the last to heat up. Yet another theory pointed to ocean acidification with ocean hypoxia tossed in for good measure.

Because of the blotchy pattern of the outbreaks there was also a question if whether what was being seen was actually the occurrence of multiple die-offs with distinct causes.

Adding to the intensity of the debates were many still unexplored avenues of investigation. Not the least of these was the absence as yet of a clinical description of the disease's course and characteristics.

Fortunately, aquariums had a lot more to offer the sea star investigations than mere recording of whose starfish died and whose did not. In particular, Vancouver Aquarium situated on the shores of an epidemic hot spot with its state of the art research teams was especially suited to play a critical role.

Over the last 50 years aquariums and zoos have moved dramatically away from the swashbuckling days of hunter and animal collector Frank Buck. No longer were hundreds of thousands of animals ripped out of foreign lands, transported to the United States, and traded as commodities for entertainment.

Vancouver Aquarium was founded in 1956 at the fading end of the Frank Buck "Bring'Em Back Alive" era. It became a forerunner of the modern day melded mission of research, conservation, and education that now guides most zoos and aquariums. Vancouver was the first aquarium to incorporate professional naturalists into their galleries. Early on it began reproducing and raising its own fish. And from its start it set about developing robust scientific teams.

Today, Vancouver Aquarium is an internationally renowned marine science center engaging in marine mammal rescue, biodiversity field surveys, a fishing gear disentanglement program, and partnering with government and conservation groups in formulating the area's marine public policy.

It was this coupling of a modern marine research center with a classic aquarium that put the institution at the forefront for working out the clinical aspects of the disease.

As a classic aquarium Vancouver had a long-term population of a dozen species of sea stars that were daily attended by professional aquarists. Some of these aquarists had been caring for the same stars for 20 to 30 years. They maintained detailed records of each sea star's histories and habits. With their logs of the stars' daily diet, the chemistry of the water they inhabited, their individual habits, and their interactions with other species, these sea star guardians likely accumulated more personal data on these pampered invertebrates than most human parents have for their own kids.

Given the premium placed on all its inhabitants the aquarium also had a long standing, dozen strong, veterinary staff to keep them healthy. The team of veterinarians, students, and technicians was led by Dr. Martin Haulena, one of the first 11 Canadian veterinarians to become board certified in the burgeoning aquatic medicine specialty.

In the fall of 2013, when the aquarium sea stars became sick Haulena and his team were called in to take on what would be a unique task among the sea star investigators. His primary job, likely heretofore uncontemplated in the annals of medical literature, was to make the sick and dying starfish well.

There's a riddle that veterinary students have been rakishly kicking around for ages.

Question: What's the difference between a physician and a veterinarian?
Answer: A physician is a veterinarian who can only treat one species.

As an aquatic medicine specialist Marty Haulena takes the joke to the extreme. What it means for his in-house day-to-day work is that he's responsible for the health, diagnostics, and treatment of literally thousands of species. His patients run from one end of the evolutionary tree to the other and on out to all of its branches minus the humans.

Some of his patients have four-chambered hearts, namely the whales, seals, otters, and other marine mammals. Some have three-chambered hearts, like the amphibians. Then there is the multitude of fishes, all of which have two-chambered hearts.

Squid and octopi have a whole other approach to oxygenating their systems. They have multiple hearts, three to be exact; two separate hearts for pumping blood through the gills, and one for pumping blood throughout the body.

And then there are the lowly ones with no heart at all, the starfish species among them, Haulena's beleaguered patients of the day.

Though Haulena had never before been called on to treat these hardy creatures he was quick to defend them. They may not have a heart, he notes, but they do have at least three and up to five distinct circulatory systems, depending on how tightly the term is defined. At the very least they have a hydraulic water vascular system for controlling locomotion in their hundreds of tube feet, a blood lymphatic vascular system akin to ours, and a coelemic (main body cavity) vascular system for their digestion.

Like most veterinarians who daily confront the dazzling variations on nature's physiologic themes Haulena practices 'comparative medicine'. This means working from the common phenomena basic to disease in all species while using the evolutionary relationships as a guide for working with the differences. It's an approach that's particularly needed when treating species for which the medical literature is as yet mostly uncharted.

For example, says Haulena, when treating sea lions for which the medical literature is still in early stages, one starts by falling back on the much more extensive medical knowledge that exists for dogs, as both the sea lion and dog are in the same suborder of carnivores.

For the sea stars, he admits, it gets "a little more challenging". This is because there's precious little medical knowledge on marine invertebrates of any kind. In any case, he adds, the key to successful comparative medicine is that "you have to observe and modify very quickly". His huge advantage, he says, are the aquarium's impressive teams of varied in-house and collaborating specialists. His first step is to consult them, starting with the question, "Is this behavior normal or not?" With the sick and dying sea stars the answer was unequivocal, "No, not normal, far from it".

From there, Haulena's approach to the critically ill stars is a mix of modern public health techniques, country doctoring, and wide ranging collaborations. Early on Haulena and his team went out with divers to observe the illness in the wild. Dr. Jeff Marliave, head of the aquarium's science teams, relates that when divers brought up sea stars displaying the disease's signature gooey lesions the first thing Haulena wanted to do was smell them. Haulena laughs at the story, but says, "Medicine as always is as much art as science. You have to use all your senses."

Another early task was the standard practice of scraping tissue samples from both the seemingly healthy and sick stars, sectioning them and sending them for laboratory analysis. Haulena put the samples in the hands of veterinary pathologist Dr. Alisa Newton at the Wildlife Conservation Society in New York. The organization is an arm of the Bronx zoo with one of the foremost veterinary labs of the Americas. Their pathology team is renowned for making the connection in the early 2000s between dying crows in New York City and the baffling disease being seen in the area's hospitals among humans. The team also identified that pathogen, until then unseen in the U.S, as the West Nile Virus.

Haulena's team also had the aquarium videographer make a time lapse video of a sea star that had begun showing the first visible white lesions characteristic of the wasting disease. The video compressed seven hours into one minute. In that time, literally overnight, the star can be seen completely coming apart, its limbs falling off and scattering around the container.

It's tempting to say the video confirmed the anecdotal evidence that the disease could run its ravaging course in less than a day. Haulena cautions, however, that there's a caveat with every clue. "Since we didn't yet have diagnostic markers for the disease, we can't be sure that what this starfish died from is the same sea star wasting being reported." Even more mind bending, since sea stars are capable of regenerating a whole new body from one limb, he says, you can't even really fix a time of death.

With so many of the aquarium stars in so many species literally dying before their eyes the team couldn't idly stand by waiting for histology results to provide clues for a course of action. Haulena and team embarked on another time-honored medical practice, diagnosis by treatment.

The stars' fulminating lesions made antibiotics the obvious place to start. However, it wasn't known if sea stars and other echinoderms could even uptake these drugs into their systems, let alone metabolize and use them. It's the perennial challenge of science, says Haulena, "You ask one of these questions and right away 100 more get generated." He assigned his veterinary resident, Dr. Brianne Phillips, and veterinary intern, Dr. Justin Rosenberg, to design experiments that would address the drug related questions as quickly as possible.

To their surprise, the sea stars did uptake the antibiotics into their tissues. In fact, they produced the same metabolites of the drug one would see in mammals given the same drug. The starfish, however, didn't respond and get well. Normally one would conclude the pathogen was not a bacterium, but so little was as yet known of starfish disease, bacteria could not be definitively ruled out.

The team anxiously waited for the histology.

For Haulena, the new connections and collaborations with researches across far flung fields and borders was the beauty of the sea star work. It was "thrilling", he says, "It was a collaboration that went viral!" But it also presented a problem.

"Traditionally there's been a disconnect between marine biologists, ecologists, and vets. That's been bridged a lot in work with the charismatic animals. It started with the group, the Gorilla Doctors, made up of multidisciplinary teams, including locals and government entities in Rwanda and the Congo, a group that has succeeded in pulling the mountain gorillas back from impending extinction. Now, also, there is this kind of collaboration with marine mammals, including bringing in the physical scientists, too. But with marine invertebrates it's been totally lacking."

"One of my favorite parts of the sea star work," says Haulena, "was seeing that all change and how much people cared. Twenty or 30 years ago that wouldn't have been the case. The fact that people cared is a sign of how far we've come."

At the same time, the spontaneous collaborations reaching out in all new directions were frustrating. There were no common mechanisms or protocols for such collaborations. "To me what was lacking was an actual physical place where there were resources devoted to sampling aquatic animals, taking the tissues, treating them appropriately, doing some of the preliminary investigations including histology and pathology on site, and then distributing the information in a coordinated way."

"Instead we had these bottlenecks because everyone is very, very busy." People couldn't just drop everything. They had to squeeze the sea star work into the rare down times in the busy jobs they already had. The always-in-demand high-tech equipment had to be scheduled for off-hours. Then there were exasperating delays in the most mundane steps, says Haulena, like trying to get the samples across borders.

"The terrestrial guys really got this," says Haulena. "There's a fantastic national wildlife health center in Madison, Wisconsin that's at the forefront of responding to these emerging terrestrial diseases. But the aquatic isn't there yet."

Finally, the histology slides arrived back from New York. The slides of the healthy sea star tissues all showed the pleasing architectural beauty of ordered cells aligned according to function. The slides of the sick stars showed the rupture and ravage of disease; the scattered necrotized cells, the broken boundaries of form, the edema, and the inundation of tissues throughout with inflammatory cells.

What the sick tissues did not show was any sign of bacteria, protozoa, or other parasitic organisms. Still, at the very least, they could now finally rule out this set of microbes as the cause.

Haulena's team, in highly gratifying collaborations with partners new and old, had identified the developmental stages of the disease, ruled out a bacterial or protozoa pathogen, and made ground breaking findings on drug responses in sea stars and urchins.

But, says Haulena with barely suppressed disappointment, "There was no smoking gun."

It wasn't just the difficulty identifying the pathogen that was keeping the scientists up at night. Questions about the consequences to the marine ecosystem of such widespread disease and about the potential for recovery were being just as urgently pursued and presenting as many stumbling blocks along the way.

5

Recovery's an Open Question
–Dr. John Pearse
Professor Emeritus, UC Santa Cruz, Ecology and Evolutionary Biology

Dr. John Pearse *(photo, Tim Stephens)*

THE SEA STAR story is full of ironies. Dr. John Pearse's career spans a lot of them.

Though recently retired after 40 years as professor of Biology at UC Santa Cruz, Dr. Pearse maintains a keen eye on all things echinoderm. Echinoderms are the class of sea creatures that include sea urchins, starfish, sea cucumbers and other marine invertebrates characterized most notably by their radial symmetry.

He writes papers, presents power points, and guides a young people's citizen science program called LiMPETS. With touching paternal affection until the Fall of 2013, Pearse cared for a laboratory full of starfish, some of which he'd been nurturing for over 30 years. But in the Fall of 2013, the starfish in laboratories and aquaria that drew water from the sea, Pearse's included, were stricken by the epidemic and died. For Pearse, it was a sorrowful personal loss.

Nonetheless, Pearse proclaims the unfolding of this starfish wasting event to be "fascinating". For one thing, he says, it's an unparalleled natural experiment to test the trophic cascade theory.

The trophic cascade theory and the keystone species theory are twin core concepts of modern ecology. They were first proposed in 1969 by American zoologist Robert Paine. Together, these concepts have quite literally turned our understanding of nature upside down.

"We used to think of top predators," says Pearse, "as just nasty things that destroyed our wonderful world. But Robert Paine's work shifted that."

What Paine proposed is that in any ecosystem there is usually a keystone species, usually the top predator, that has an outsized influence in maintaining a healthy balance in its ecosystem. If for any reason that top predator is removed from the environment, claims the theory, a trophic cascade is triggered, i.e. a system wide collapse and loss of species.

The theory explains that removal of the top predator from a natural community results in an explosive increase of mid-sized prey on which the top predator feeds. That inflated population of mid-sized prey then over-forages, essentially consuming their whole food supply. This leads to their starvation or disease among the mid-sized animals, and ultimately to their death. The end result is that the balance of the whole system is thrown so out of whack that multiple species exterminations result.

There are numerous examples of mechanisms through which keystone species act as linchpins in ecosystems. Sea otters, for example, were once believed to be the bane of abalone fishermen because the sea otters ate abalone. Under the keystone species concept, it's now understood that sea otters, far from being noxious competitors, were controlling the number of kelp-eating sea urchins. In so doing, the otter's key role in maintaining healthy kelp beds outweighs its predation on abalone. In fact, it leads to an overall increase in the number of abalone, a theoretical prediction borne out in experiment.

Similarly, mountain lions, once thought by hunters to be pernicious competitors for deer, are now understood to be essential for maintaining healthy deer populations. In the eastern United States where mountain lions have been exterminated, the deer populations have exploded. That imbalance has resulted in a rampant increase in many serious diseases afflicting humans and wildlife, diseases borne by deer ticks.

In contrast, in the western United States there are a number of healthy populations of mountain lions. Their behavior illustrates another mechanism by which an apex predator can support its ecosystem: these mountain lions put on regular feasts for all. Studies of their kills find that once sated the mountain lion moves off and a multitude of the system's wildlife, from bears to skunks, foxes, ravens, eagles, owls, and more, move in for effortless dining compliments of the host.

The keystone theory, however, is most dramatically illustrated by what happens when top predators that have been missing from an environment are reintroduced into their degraded ecosystems. For example, in astonishingly few years after the top predator wolves were returned to Yellowstone National Park, the bison on which the wolf feeds were spurred out of their sedentary overgrazing habits and were once again enlivened to be on the move. The overgrazed meadows and riparian zones of Yellowstone stunned biologists by the speed with which they revegetated. A rich array of plants and animals that had previously disappeared with the loss of the wolves quickly repopulated the area. Similarly, degraded stream ecosystems blossom back to a dazzling diversity of life when keystone beavers are reintroduced.

One of the great ironies in the sea star story is that the original work by Robert Paine that led him to formulating the keystone species theory was done on the ocher sea star, the same star in the same Pacific tide pools that has been one of the species most afflicted by the epidemic.

The precious ochre star, every kids' tide pool delight, is also a predator, a top predator, the veritable wolf of its watery intertidal world. It is this fact that has scientists so intensely worried about the potential coast wide consequences of the sea star demise.

In his seminal experiment, one that would likely be frowned on today, Paine removed the ochre stars from selected rocks at Washington's Olympic peninsula. He soon observed an explosion of mussels on which the sea star feeds. The overpopulation of mussels then drove out other species leading to the collapse of the intertidal system around those rocks. It's the coast wide demise of this same ochre star that for better or worse is going to give the keystone theory its most extensive testing to date.

In so doing, it's hoped there will be insights into how the trophic cascade either does or does not manifest in a wide spectrum of marine environments. Such information could greatly enhance and nuance the management and conservation of marine coastal zones.

John Pearse wholehearted supports the long-term big data gathering by MARINe that's making it possible to answer so many of the urgent questions surrounding the disease and its ecologic consequences. "I hate to say it," says Pearse, "but the sea star wasting event was a blessing for MARINe and PISCO because suddenly they have proof they're relevant." (PISCO is the fisheries big data project, a sister project of the MARINe intertidal project.)

"Before when they were doing these studies," says Pearse, "sure they were mapping data, but other than that they didn't have anything to show for it. A number of people," he says, "were beginning to wonder if all that money was worth it. But as a result of all that data and mapping, when the starfish event occurred, they were on it. You wouldn't have known about it otherwise."

Then, in a more wistful mood, Pearse expresses an entirely different view of his beloved marine science. He bemoans the loss today of what he longingly and lovingly refers to as "curiosity science". "Studying the natural history, the basic life cycle biology of an animal, building your own equipment, following your curiosity, training your observations..." His voice goes quiet before resuming. The big data, big computers, and big tech science, he goes on to explain, have stigmatized curiosity science as vestigial before its time. The "curiosity science", he says, is now all but impossible to fund.

Probably the most stinging irony of the sea star wasting event is the gaping holes in knowledge that Pearse's 'curiosity science' might have answered in what he wryly refers to as his "wrong track career". As the effort to map the spread of the disease wound down, focus turned to questions of causation, recovery, and environmental factors. But time and again those gaps left investigators groping in the blind spots around starfish biology.

The really basic stuff. Just for one example, says Pearse, "It's not known how to determine the age of a starfish, though it is possible to age a sea urchin, a close relative of starfish. Sea urchins are known to reach 75 to 100 years of age or more. I think they're immortal, actually," says Pearse of both urchins and starfish, "I don't think they undergo senility and die of old age. They die of bad luck, sooner or later something's going to get them."

Now in light of the sea star disease this seemingly trifling question of determining the age of sea stars has suddenly become of urgent importance to understanding the recovery potential of the whole west coast marine environment.

Two years after the starfish disease was first reported, a contagious excitement swept over researchers as reports came in that droves of baby starfish were being found along the coast. News media were ecstatic as well. Headlines cheered the hope of recovery.

Pearse, however, is still far from convinced. Is this bumper crop of tiny starfish the offspring of the few that adults that survived the epidemic and, as such, cause for celebration that even a few remaining adults can repopulate a recovery?

Or, as Pearse thinks more likely, were these 'babies' actually spawned a year or more before the epidemic and they simply survived the disease in a non-vulnerable free floating larval phase as the disease lay waste to the adults? If that's the case, as these babies mature will they now likely also become vulnerable and die?

The daunting dilemma is that without knowing how to determine the age of the 'babies' those critical questions can't be answered. It's just one of the vexing fundamental knowledge gaps that leads to Pearse's ominous view that "recovery is an open question."

As a young Stanford doctoral student in biology in the 1960s, Pearse volunteered to assist on a research project in Antarctica. The question the team was hoping to answer was whether reproduction in marine invertebrates was triggered by light or by temperature. Antarctica was chosen as an ideal site to tease out the answer because marine temperature there is a virtual constant.

Once on site, this wasn't exactly what Pearse had envisioned in his youthful enthusiasm for desert biology growing up in Arizona. Huddled in parka and gloves down at the bottom of the earth he found himself building traps in the blasted cold, digging holes through the desolate ice, and seeing what the traps would catch.

The very first creatures to come into his traps were starfish. Due perhaps to the bleak and barren circumstances of his surroundings, the starfish in turn caught Pearse's fancy. "So I said, well, I'll work on them." He

followed up by doing his doctoral thesis on the reproduction of starfish and has been working with starfish
up to his retirement in 2014 and beyond. A passionate
naturalist to the core John Pearse still can't give up his
fascination with unanswered questions about basic starfish biology.

Many of the facts we do know about starfish are thanks
to the Pearse's life work, and many of the questions that
bedevil the epidemic investigators are questions Pearse
has raised. Starfish are broadcast spawners, though it's
not known whether their spawning is triggered by each
other, by stress, or by other environmental factors.

The young are free floating until they settle onto the
bottom, though the timing isn't known. No one, he says,
has been able to raise starfish in the lab through a full
life cycle. He does believe though that it takes three or
four years for starfish to reach sexual maturity. And he
knows it is these basic unanswered reproductive questions that are so critical to understanding starfish recovery from this devastating disease.

"All in all, we're not even close now to describing the
biology of this species." Adding to the void is the fact that
echinoderms have no skeletons and don't leave good fossils to help fill in the blanks. But in order to do the kind
of curiosity science necessary to explore those questions,
says Pearse, "You almost have to get out of academia."

Then, returning to a lighter mood, John Pearse expresses a lot of faith in his marine biologist colleagues.

He believes that their zeal and curiosity will persist. After all, he says, none of them went into it for the money or academic fame.

6

We'd Darn Well Better Figure Out What's Going On–Dr. Drew Harvell

Professor of Ecology and Evolutionary Biology, Cornell University

Dr. Drew Harvell, *(photo, Cornell University)*

LOOKING BACK AT the titles of Dr. Drew Harvell's research papers from a decade and a half before the starfish event you'd swear she was peering into a crystal ball.

In 1999 Harvell was the lead author of a paper titled *Emerging Marine Diseases--Climate Links and Anthropogenic Factors.* In 2002, following a handful of intervening papers, she published *Climate Warming and Disease Risks for Terrestrial and Marine Biota.*

It's remarkable that Harvell published these papers at a time when if anyone thought of marine diseases at all it was in regard to fish farms, aquaria, hatcheries, or hobbies. Marine wildlife diseases were barely on the radar, and for the most part were considered inconsequential. It was also a time when scientists had only recently reached consensus on climate change, and years before Al Gore's 2006 movie, An Inconvenient Truth, would try to convince the world that climate change was real.

Then, in 2004, Harvell published *The Rising Tide of Ocean Diseases, Unsolved Problems and Research Priorities.* In nine tightly written pages, she pulls together her growing knowledge of marine wildlife diseases and outlines the reasons disease processes in the ocean likely have significant differences from diseases processes on land. One of her sweeping insights is that there is a greater diversity of hosts and pathogens in the oceans with most of the hosts being invertebrates. Another is that ocean food chains are longer than on land and disease spread rates are extremely rapid.

From these fundamental differences in the organization of life at sea she surmises that responding to ocean disease may require revamping of the methods and models of land side epidemiology, preventions and treatments.

It would be still another decade before the sea star epidemic would bring the full significance of Harvell's ideas to the fore.

There's a dazzling allure to the leap of knowledge that occurs when a scientist uses seemingly disparate observations and synthesizes them into coherent new ways of understanding the world. From the outside it can appear that the scattered pieces of a puzzle have come together as if by magic.

From the inside the alchemy of scientific insight is exasperatingly more complicated, demanding, and in the last analysis, all the more awesome because of it. Igniting the process usually takes a very smart mind landing on a lot of the right places at all the right times. Harvell certainly covered all those bases.

In graduate school at the University of Washington, Harvell was fortunate to study under Robert Paine. As already noted it was Paine who pioneered the breakthrough ecological concepts of keystone species and trophic cascades. Not surprisingly these topics were the core of his class discussions, with emphasis on how these phenomena unfolded in marine environments.

After graduating with her doctorate, Harvell chose to study defense mechanisms of Caribbean corals. As fate would have it, this was right at the time when these corals were being massively attacked by disease, and just as the scientific literature was beginning to unravel the role of the oceans in mediating the effects of climate change.

"Corals were the first ecosystem hit really hard by climate warming," says Harvell. It was Harvell's early research that established that linkage and delivered the sobering news with scientific rigor. "These coral diseases," she says, "became the first posterchild for climate change endangering a whole ecosystem." Polar bears, she adds, were not yet on the radar as victims of global warming, though they followed close behind.

Princeton University animal disease expert Andy Dodson recognized the profound implications of Harvell's work. He invited her to meet with and join a group of scientists working on the ecology of infectious disease.

Previously, virtually all the scientists attending these meetings were studying land animal diseases. Mixing in researchers on marine diseases with the land people set interdisciplinary sparks flying. Many members in the group stopped seeing disease as an isolated problem in the particular ecosystem on which they were working. They came to realize that, "'Oh, these disease outbreaks are a problem across all these systems.'" These seminal discussions would eventually contribute to a more recent breakthrough in ecology - the inclusion of disease as a key factor in the dynamics of all ecosystems, whether healthy and perturbed.

At the time, however, says Harvell, "We were all dealing with more disease outbreaks than we had any way of handling. Just seeing that made it really clear to me this was going to be a big problem." It was those meetings in the early 2000s that fueled Harvell's focus on probing the links between global warming and marine disease outbreaks.

But it takes more than a sharp mind at the right places and times before new ideas get fully adopted. The science doesn't take root without arduous testing every alternative hypotheses one can think of. A researcher must raise the challenging questions every step of the way and be prepared to work on those by others in the field. That demanding process can take years of a scientist's life.

On that score, too, Harvell had the necessary academic grit. In the 15 years between her early papers on marine wildlife diseases and the 2013 outbreak of sea star wasting disease, Harvell authored and co-authored over 100 original research publications. Her prodigious work was motivated by the science community's growing alarm for the planet and her own intense determination to understand what was happening.

There was another stepping-stone Harvell had set in place just prior to the sea star epidemic. In 2011, sensing a need to stretch the meaning of 'interdisciplinary' to new limits, Harvell teamed up with a professor of resource economics, Jon Conrad, and a professor of communication, Katherine McComas. Together, they started the Ecology of Infectious Marine Diseases Research Coordination Network. It was a network that would prove as critical to the sea star work as the Pete Raimondi's MARINe, and the more so when the two networks would soon join forces.

By the time of the first flare ups of the sea star epidemic Harvell's network had 50 members. Among them was Dr. Ian Hewson, a marine virologist and a professor colleague of Harvell's at Cornell University, and Paul Hershberger, a fisheries biologist, head of Morrowstone Marine Station, the Northwest's premier fisheries lab. Both would play critical roles in the work to come.

The stars really couldn't have been better aligned, nor Harvell and her network better prepared, to finally nail down the mysterious sea star pathogen that had eluded so many others. Indeed, when the disease reports started coming in Harvell says without hesitation, "It didn't come as a surprise that this happened."

What did shock her, she says, was the number of species affected, the geographic scope, and the virulence. "The wide host range, that's the part that's really rotten about this, that's the most vexing part of the whole thing." It's extremely rare that a disease suddenly jumps over to 20 or more species as did the sea star wasting disease.

"There had been a small sea star event two years before this one," says Harvell. "We missed getting those samples so when this event started it was a clear priority for me." The fact that this event was killing ecologically important keystone species added even more to the urgency she imparted to her lab.

Harvell's lab was already going full steam on multiple other marine diseases. But when the starfish disease hit she told her team, "We'd darn well better figure out what is going on!" The pressure became almost too intense for some of her researchers to handle. "I had a postdoctoral student almost quit," says Harvell. "The postdoc said, 'Would you just settle down, we have time to do this'. I said, 'No, we don't'."

Despite the extensive expertise of her marine disease network, identifying the pathogen that had eluded so many others soon proved to be anything but smooth sailing.

"Early signs were that the pathogen was so virulent," says Harvell, "I wasn't willing to do any experiments in the lab at Friday Harbor", the West Coast lab where Harvell carried out the bulk of her marine field work. "We had some level of biological quarantine security at the facility, but not enough. The last thing I wanted was to fuel the spread."

What she and her team were able to do right away was to collect samples and send them to Ian Hewson, her colleague back at Cornell University in New York. "It was incredibly important that we had someone like Ian," says

Harvell, "a real virologist studying echinoderms, probably the only guy in the world doing that. It was incredibly fortunate having him at Cornell."

The first question they had for Hewson was whether they were dealing with a bacterium or a virus. The answer that came back confirmed Marty Haulena's findings that the pathogen was not a bacterium and was most likely a virus. That fact opened Pandora's box.

A 2013 article in The Scientist magazine claims there are likely 100 million times more viruses on earth than there are stars in the universe, most of which viruses are in the ocean. One of the few things known about marine viruses is that in a drop of surface sea water there are over 10 million viruses, the overwhelming majority of which have not yet been identified. Harvell's own work had dealt mostly with bacterial and fungal pathogens. Adding to the complexities were recent findings that marine viruses often differ from land viruses in unexpected ways. There are marine 'giant viruses', and other marine viruses that infect these giant viruses. Another characteristic of many marine viruses, in contrast to most terrestrial viruses, is that they tend not to be host specific.

At the same time that scientists were becoming aware of the massive unknowns about marine viruses, they were also beginning to realize that these viruses en masse are heavy hitters in regulating the earth's carbon cycles. As such, they have a profound impact on climate, and conversely, climate likely has a profound impact on the viruses. When these viruses infect their microbial marine hosts over the enormous areas and depths of the seas, the infected micro-organisms rupture, releasing untold amounts of carbon back into the sea, instead of, as previously thought, all that carbon being moved up and sequestered in the food chain.

It was into this cauldron of marine virus conjecture that Harvell and team set out in search of the one infinitesimal sea star pathogen. Luckily, the first questions that needed to be answered followed well established lines, as did the method needed to answer them - demonstrate by injection that a virus pathogen is indeed associated with the disease.

To start the laboratory investigation, sick sea stars are thoroughly macerated in a super-blender. All particles larger than a virus are filtered out. Some of the remaining residue is then injected into healthy sea stars to see if the healthy stars become infected. Another batch of residue, the control, is heat treated to kill the viruses before it too is injected into healthy sea stars.

Once it can be shown that only the live viral soup results in healthy stars becoming sick at the very least you know you've got the culprit in the test tube – albeit along with the legions of other non-pathogenic viruses that can be found on all healthy organisms, including sea stars. The next trick is to find the needle in the haystack, the one pathogenic virus among the millions.

Harvell got past the first hurdle. She had found a lab that had both the necessary bio-security for working with high-risk pathogens and the lab's willingness to undertake the injection experiments. It clearly helped that the head of the Morrowstone Marine Field Station in Washington State was fishery biologist Paul Hershberger, a member of Harvell's marine disease network.

Of the 20 or more species affected, the sunflower star was by far most susceptible which was why the team chose it for the injection experiments. As always, a batch of healthy stars was needed to serve as the experiment's controls. "I was worried the epidemic was sweeping through them so fast," says Harvell, "that we wouldn't have time to do the experiment before all our hosts became infected."

Then next problem Harvell's team had to grapple with was that the sunflower stars were too big for the tanks.

But the most exasperating obstacle was money. "I knew it was going to be a long hard road to get funding. Unfortunately there's not much funding because there's really, really big questions that urgently need to be answered. We talked with a couple foundations and the funds didn't come through. I would have done a lot more if I had the money, but we also had active research underway on eelgrasses. We couldn't just throw everything else aside."

Harvell estimates that the total value of the work done by all the scientists who worked on sea star wasting syndrome was probably tens of millions of dollars, money that simply wasn't there. "They bootlegged, patched together other grants, they worked for more hours than they were paid for and they did it because they cared."

Beyond the work she was putting in to identify the sea star pathogen, there were other pressing questions Harvell was dying to investigate. "If we had the money, there's some really important work we could have done. One of the most urgent questions is understanding whether we have some resistant sea stars on our shores and what that means and how does their immune system work. I can barely talk about it," says Harvell, "because it's so upsetting we can't do that work."

But there's a sweet nectar often mixed in to science's hard drawn lines of rigorous study, tightly controlled experiments, and maddening mundane obstacles. Unexpectedly, there is pure sweet serendipity.

In the midst of her lab's feverish endeavor to finally get the experiments underway to nail down the identity of the pathogen, Harvell's phone rang. It was a call that would open a completely unanticipated new chapter in her work.

7

All the Way to the Mountaintops --Seth Dawson

**Staffer, Office of Congressman Denny Heck,
Olympia, WA**

**Seth Dawson (left) and Congressman
Denny Heck** (*photo, Kati Sills*)

BY THE SUMMER of 2014, the public's distress over the starfish had spurred literally thousands of media reports covering the sea star disease. Each in turn strengthened the bridge between the marine scientists and their communities. Scientists were being invited to forums and classrooms. Local artists memorialized the starfish in paintings. School kids took part in starfish projects. And the citizen science program pressed on.

One of the media reports found its way into the hands of an intern who worked in the office of Congressman Denny Heck, Olympia, Washington's freshman representative. The intern was so upset by the story she was reading that she brought it to the attention of staffer Seth Dawson.

The very last thing Seth Dawson ever imagined for himself was work immersed in the sciences. Throughout his youth his passions swung between tennis and progressive politics. Soon after graduating with a degree in politics and armed with job experience to back it up, he was thrilled to land a plum job as a staffer for Congressman Heck.

As in most congressional offices, a capable staffer like Dawson is assigned specific issue areas in which he or she is expected to develop expertise. This includes tracking trends on the assigned issues, advising the congressperson, shaping legislative actions, and never missing a beat. Which is where Dawson's life veered wildly into the unexpected.

The issues to which Dawson was assigned were: energy, technology, the judicial, education, space, tribal issues, natural resources, and the environment. In short, a menu that could choke a whole stable of horses.

Given the fever pitched economic growth along the Olympia-Seattle corridor there wasn't one of these issues that could be given short shrift. Dawson, however, was exactly where he wanted to be, in the thick of things – the kind of things that mattered.

There was one issue, however, that would soon put Dawson's mettle to the test. Denny Heck had made the environment a priority in his congressional campaign. Once elected it was an issue on which he quickly made bold strides. Just months into his first term Heck co-founded the congressional Puget Sound Recovery Caucus. Its ambitious goal was to enlist federal clout to (a) reverse the Sound's pollution, (b) protect and restore its habitat, and (c) re-open the Sound's shellfish beds.

One look at a map shows how thoroughly Puget Sound's broad arterial matrix of marine waterways dominates and defines the region. With its ubiquitous shorelines, this Northwest meeting of marine and mega-metropolis all but guaranteed a tower-of-babel clamoring of wildly diverse interests demanding to be heard. It's home to the likes of Boeing Aircraft, golden eagles, Starbucks Inc., protestors in kayaks, orca whales, Amazon.com, the West Coast's premier fishing fleet, and a full spectrum of environmental groups ranging from over a dozen chapters of the buttoned-down National Audubon Society to the hell-raising rogue ships of the Sea Shepherd Conservation Society.

Moreover, the starting point for the work of Congressman Heck's Recovery Caucus was a marine ecosystem already massively damaged by the area's mushrooming growth.

As point person on the project from Heck's office Dawson seemed to be steadying his grip in the maelstrom by portraying his role in a staccato burst of words. "It's incredibly complicated. Everything is interconnected. All the way to the mountaintops!"

Perhaps in dedication to the mission or in utter surrender to its shapeshifting girth, when the intern came in that summer and presented Dawson with the article profiling the starfish plight, Dawson didn't miss a beat. He immediately rose to the challenge.

His first step was to ask his Puget Sound contacts as to who were the major players among the scientists working on the starfish situation.

Major player list in hand, Dawson made his first call to Drew Harvell. When Harvell answered, Dawson opened the conversation with a question that would be celestial music to any constituent's ears. "What do you need government to be doing?" he asked.

Not surprisingly, despite being stretched to capacity by the demands of her lab work, Harvell didn't miss a beat either. Right away she saw the potential for tackling some of the most frustrating obstacles that had plagued her and other scientists in responding to the sea star disease. And so too, when called, did Pete Raimondi at UC Santa Cruz. Together, they wasted no time forging a legislative answer not just for better responding to the sea star emergency but for responding to all future marine diseases outbreaks.

Most interestingly, instead of trying to adapt existing protocols from the Centers for Disease Control for disease outbreaks in humans, or lifting existing wildlife protocols for terrestrial animals, the team recognized what Harvell had posited over a decade ago. Marine diseases require responses tailored to their distinct environment.

The ad hoc team reached into their experience. After all, Harvell and Raimondi had their collective insights and detailed wish lists from the sea star epidemic on the tip of their tongues. And now they had the enthusiastic legislative guidance of Seth Dawson.

The process of drafting the bill was lightning fast. In a matter of months, on September 18, 2014, Congressperson Denny Heck introduced the Marine Disease Emergency Act to Congress. Along the way, it gathered six legislative co-sponsors from the three Western Coastal states.

The Marine Disease Emergency Act would establish:

A federal mechanism for declaring a marine disease emergency, designating an emergency coordinator, and specifying the timing and steps for action to be triggered by that declaration. It further establishes that

(1) —Not later than 28 days after declaring a marine disease emergency under this section the Secretary [of Commerce] shall, in consultation with the Task Force, develop a written response plan for such emergency based on sound science. Including "at minimum"

(A) a list of persons at appropriate Federal, regional, State, and local agencies who can assist the Secretary in implementing a coordinated and effective response to the marine disease emergency;

(B) a description of the steps necessary to diagnose the cause of the marine disease emergency;

(C) training, mobilization, and utilization procedures for personnel, facilities, and other resources necessary to conduct a rapid and effective response to the marine disease emergency;

(D) an assessment of the potential effects of the marine disease emergency on populations of marine species;

(E) strategies to minimize morbidity and mortality in marine species and minimize transmission of the disease; and

(F) provisions to protect other populations of aquacultured animals, plants, marine mammals, and birds that could be directly or indirectly impacted by the marine disease emergency or response actions.

The bill also called for establishing

- A national data repository to facilitate the development, coordination, and rapid dissemination of marine disease research,
- A permanent, volunteer "Marine Disease Working Group" to advise the Secretary of Commerce on marine disease emergencies,

And in welcome relief from the long, exasperating, fruitless searches for money, the Marine Disease Emergency Act would create…

- A "Marine Disease Emergency Fund" within the Treasury Department
    A full text of the bill can be seen here:
    www.congress.gov/bill/114th-congress/house-bill/936/text

None of the team that came together to forge the bill expected it would be passed the first year. The hope was it would be a platform for educating politicians to the threat of marine diseases and to the need for coordinated response at the federal level.

And exactly as hoped, by February of 2015, when the bill would be reintroduced to the next congressional session, the Marine Disease Emergency Act had gathered 13 bipartisan and bi-coastal co-sponsors, doubling the number supporting the bill just months before.

On February 13, 2015, Denny Heck stood before Congress, pulled a starfish out of his pocket, held it up before his colleagues and reintroduced the act. The team understood that there still wasn't much chance yet of it actually being passed into law. They were already speculating that its ultimate success would likely begin by winning approval in coastal state legislatures.

For now, however, the bill had succeeded in at least one important way. It had strengthened a vital bridge between the scientists and politicians. It wouldn't be long before the marine disease scientists themselves who would be making their way to Washington. Of all the mighty and mythic creatures that grace the seas, it's worth a moment to ponder that it was the petite and priceless starfish paving the way.

8

Down the Rabbit Hole, Into the Spotlight–Dr. Ian Hewson
Associate Professor, Cornell University, Department of Microbiology

Dr. Ian Hewson *(photo, Cornell University)*

Part 1 ~ Down the Rabbit Hole...

IN ITS RIGOROUS search for new knowledge the scientific method aims to remove all forms of human bias. So it's understandable that the public often harbors an image of scientists as aloof, austere, and devoid of cheer. It may come as a surprise how many scientists get a thrill out of their work and how often they describe their time in the lab as fun. That would certainly be the case for Ian Hewson, who as a professor at landlocked Cornell University in upstate New York is happy as a clam diving ever deeper into the hidden universe of marine microbes.

It's also a common misapprehension that immersion in their esoteric worlds renders scientists absent minded with respect to the everyday nuances of family and friends. Again, to the contrary, like most scientists and humans all, Hewson is devoted to his robust family life, and rarely more urgently so than just as he was coming up on the final deadline for submission of his paper - the really big one - laying out his findings on the sea star disease.

Of the many publications in Hewson's young career this one carried the pressure of claiming a high profile breakthrough. Hewson and his team were about to announce the identity of the one ocean virus among gazillions they found to be associated with the sea star disease. Every word of this paper had to line up as precisely as the sequence of a genetic code.

Adding to the pressure was the fact that unlike most scientific papers which typically list three or four co-authors, Hewson was listing an unheard of throng of 25 other scientists as co-authors. He says he believes in giving full intellectual credit to all who contribute. In regard to the early sea star work that laid the foundation for his own team's findings, Hewson wanted to accurately represent the extraordinary collaboration that had taken place across distance and disciplines.

Putting that sentiment into practice, however, was coming down to the crunch. The days before final submission of the paper were the last chance for each of these 25 co-authors to speak their piece on the final wording, as each and every one was wont to do. Hewson is able to enjoy a good laugh about it now, but at the time he says, "It was crazy!" Herding cats didn't begin to describe the task of bringing everyone together on a coherent whole.

The electricity around the upcoming paper was being even further amped up by the press. Tuned in as they were to each new development in the sea star story reporters had easily picked up on the rumors of Hewson's findings. They were already tracking down leads and jockeying for angles. Hewson also had to convince his 25 co-authors to keep a lid on the story until the paper was actually in print.

Such was the daunting burden of last-minute ordeals Hewson carried with him as he boarded a hurriedly arranged flight from Ithica, New York half-way round the world to Melbourne, Australia. He was headed back to his homeland with heavy heart to visit his father whose health had suddenly turned for the worse. When it came to his father the pressures of work-related events didn't matter.

It was his father, says Hewson, who had awakened his love of the sciences. An agricultural development specialist in the Australian diplomatic corps, Hewson's father had spent endless hours doing science experiments with his eager young son.

There were other perks too for a youngster having both parents in the diplomatic corps. The best, says Hewson, was when the family was stationed in Kenya. There, 11-year-old kids were allowed to take SCUBA diving lessons, something that would never have been permitted in their Australian homeland. A few dives into the underwater world, combined with the love of science instilled by his father, and a marine scientist was in the making.

Hewson's childhood travels from country to country had also nurtured his delight in venturing off on his own into uncharted territory. In 1998, scouting around for an undergraduate honors project at the University of Queensland, Hewson couldn't find one paper written on marine viruses. There was hardly any awareness at all that viruses even existed in the marine environment, says Hewson, and that's what drew him to his thesis topic on estuary viruses.

Following his postdoctoral work at UC Santa Cruz, Hewson has a decidedly more mundane explanation for his career move to Cornell University where he was surrounded on every horizon by a sea of upstate New York truck farms. As distinguished an institution as Cornell is, to this day it has no formal marine science department and not a whiff of salt in its air. Hewson's motive, however, will be all too familiar to many. "After graduating," he says, "I needed a job."

Despite the distance from salt water it's all worked out splendidly to Hewson's liking. There's an informal core group of a half dozen marine scientists there who provide collegiality. Students can get a solid grounding in the subject if that's their interest. And just as important, says Hewson, the atmosphere at Cornell has been eminently supportive of the marine work.

The timing of his career focus on marine microbes was also propitious. During the 1990's and throughout the last decade the field of marine microbiology exploded. The boom was fueled, he says, by two major drivers each one boosting the other. One was the nascent recognition of the formidable role of marine microorganisms in the carbon cycle of the earth. These vast watery fields of microbes absorb the dissolved carbon dioxide in the upper ocean, sequester it, and transport it to the deep ocean as they die. Not surprisingly, the significance of that recognition has been immeasurably amplified by the growing concern over climate change.

The second and parallel driver of the advances was the development of the technology needed to study these microbes; namely the advent of computers capable of handling the big data of an organism's molecular genetics.

However, Hewson notes, by 2013 there was still a monumental divide that hadn't been breached between those dealing with microbes as pathogens and those dealing with the non-pathology side, such as microbes' role in carbon cycling. "It was a very different crowd of investigators." There were pathologists and veterinarians in one camp and the bio oceanographers in another. They weren't opposed in any way, but they weren't cross pollinating either. "They were two very different crowds who prior to 2013 never held conferences together."

Even within the marine pathogen camp, as Cornell colleague Drew Harvell noted earlier, by the time of the sea star disease, Ian Hewson was likely the only one in the world with expertise on marine virus pathogens that infected echinoderms. Hewson himself, however, doesn't see his rarefied knowledge as out of the ordinary of what scientists everywhere are doing every day. "You're always going down the rabbit hole with science", he says.

Once alerted to the catastrophic dimensions of the sea star disease, like the other scientists involved, Hewson launched a feverish and frustrating search for quick response money to support the needed work. He counts himself as one of the lucky ones. Hewson was ultimately able to obtain a whopping $22,000 from the National Science Foundation, funds that were earmarked to test 10 starfish for bacterial and viral loads. He laughs again in hindsight. "Half that money went to Fed Ex for transporting the coolers with samples that were coming in from Friday Harbor and the Olympic National Park."

Like the others, he says, "There was a lot of volunteering. I didn't get any salary for that work."

Miles above the earth the unending hours crossing oceans, continents, and hemispheres while pinned motionless in his seat turned out to be a blessing in disguise. So too was the airline's open internet. In a redeye blizzard of emails back and forth with his 25 co-authors Hewson's sea star paper was being chiseled into its final form to the satisfaction of all. On August 28, 2014, the paper was received and accepted for review by the Proceedings of the National Academy of Sciences. It was approved October 21, 2014, and published on December 2, 2014.

Part 2 - Into the Spotlight

It's true. Four centuries after Francis Bacon set forth the guidelines of the modern scientific method we still have no idea how to determine the age of a starfish nor do we know what triggers its reproductive cycle. But heads up! The bio-sciences of late haven't exactly been languishing in stagnation.

The last half-century has produced breathtaking breakthroughs in molecular genetics, the leading edge of which Ian Hewson has brought to the service of the starfish cause.

The springboard for these advances can be traced back to 1952 when pioneering chemist Rosalind Franklin produced her heralded x-ray diffraction photo 51, providing the key to the double helix structure of DNA. From there, in rapid succession, came the first sequencing of RNA, followed by explosive advances in sequencing techniques that allowed for unraveling the genetic codes of ever more complex organisms. Fast forward to the international collaboration that succeeded in sequencing the entire human genome in 2007, to the present day field of genomics providing searchable mega-libraries of microbe genetics. Even more recently, and vital to the Hewson sea star work, the powerful new field of metagenomics allows for the genetic analysis of whole communities of microbes from environmental samples. Such was the legacy Hewson's paper could draw on.

Despite the bold pace of these advances each new step is made as if walking through a minefield of unknowns. So too, starting with the title, the Hewson sea star paper expresses caution. The title reads, *Densovirus associated with sea-star wasting disease and mass mortality*. It claims to identify the virus "associated with" the disease, not to assert it as cause.

No matter how strong the experimental evidence of causation no scientist wants to leave themselves open to a common mistake of logic, the one made by the rooster that concludes that it's his crowing at dawn that causes the sun to rise. We humans can all enjoy a good laugh at this poor rooster's ignorance, but mistaking correlation for causality slips again and again into our thinking. The persistence of the beliefs that Fukushima radiation must be the cause of sea star disease, or that vaccinations cause autism, are just two examples, both of which thrive on little more than coincidences of timing.

Establishing causation in any field of knowledge must meet a substantial burden of proof. Even getting to 'associated with' is a marathon of methodical thinking and experimental design. Thankfully, Hewson and co-authors took as much care in writing clearly as they did in the investigation, making the steps and findings accessible to all.

Their first step, reconfirming that the likely pathogen was virus sized and not a bacterium, was fairly simple. Bacteria are many times larger than viruses and can be seen under a standard microscope. Viruses cannot. No suspect bacteria had been found by any of the teams in the tissues of sick sea stars.

The second step, called a viral challenge test, is also an established technique. This was accomplished by the injection experiments Drew Harvell had lined up to be carried out at the Morrowstone Fisheries lab in

Washington. Symptomatic sea stars were emulsified in a super blender. The liquid was finely filtered so that all particles larger than a virus were removed. Half the filtrate was heated to kill the viruses. The other half of the filtrate containing live virus was left untreated.

The healthy sea stars injected with the untreated filtrate became sick. The healthy sea stars injected with the heat-treated filtrate remained healthy. The results were clear cut. But the experiment was repeated, this time by emulsifying the newly sick sea stars. Again, healthy stars injected with the unheated filtrate became sick. And healthy stars treated with the heated filtrate remained healthy.

This brought the authors to the point of confidence in stating, "These experiments demonstrate that the disease is transmissible from symptomatic to asymptomatic individuals and that the pathogenic agent is virus-sized (i.e., <200 nm in diameter)."

Next, knowing that any organism, healthy or not, hosts a range of viruses, the team set out to identify the one virus in the filtrate that associated with the illness. This is where metagenomics and the massive searchable genomic data banks proved indispensable. Comparison of the viruses of healthy vs sick sea stars yielded only one virus candidate present in significantly higher loads in the sick stars than the healthy stars.

Hewson and team identified the virus as a kind of densovirus, a subfamily of viruses in the family of parvoviruses.

This is a virus group familiar to dog owners. The canine parvovirus is so highly contagious and prevalent, and so frequently lethal, that most dog owners have their pets vaccinated against it. The extended family of parvoviruses encompasses a large number of pathogenic viruses, variously infecting humans, mink, pigs, cows, cats, and more, and producing a unique set of symptoms in each.

The densoviruses are a subfamily of the parvoviruses and are characterized by infecting a range of invertebrates from insects to shrimp. The particular densovirus the Hewson team identified as associated with the sea star disease was previously unknown, giving Hewson the naming rights. Not to unnecessarily exaggerate the honor, they named the virus SSaDV (sea star associated densovirus).

The work of supporting their claim however wasn't quite done. Building certainty for their conclusions required evidence that the association between the newly identified virus and the disease held up against other known characteristics of viral diseases in general and of the sea star wasting syndrome in particular.

They needed to see if the viral load of SSaDV in sick sea stars from the field was significantly higher than the viral load in healthy stars from the field. It was.

They needed to see if the viral load of SSaDV of a sick sea star increased as the sea star became sicker. It did.

And they wanted to see if there was at least a viable method of transmission through water as would be consistent with the observed speed of the disease's spread, a mode of transmission that didn't require direct contact from sick to healthy stars. They searched areas and aquaria where the disease had spread and found the SSaDV in suspended particulate matter, in sediments, and in aquaria filters. This showed the virus could be water borne.

In all, the team analyzed 330 starfish, a number far greater than the 10 sea stars Hewson's grant money was earmarked to cover.

What more then could possibly be needed to claim that the virus SSaDV was the pathogen causing the death of so many sea stars? Scientific proof of causation requires that the results obtained by one team, no matter how strongly suggestive of a cause, can be independently reproduced by other labs and other investigators. And that always takes time.

No matter, the media was ravenous to report on the Hewson findings and rightly so. Finally identifying the likely pathogen of such a virulent and widespread disease in multiple keystone and charismatic species was critically important news. That it was done in a year's time with no salaries and having to scratch for funds made it an even bigger deal. Hewson was bombarded by reporters. No fewer than 430 media outlets jumped on the story. They ranged from BBC Radio to a German Sport Diver magazine to National Geographic and many more. And it was all over social media for weeks. "It was an exciting opportunity to spread the word," says Hewson.

Despite all the fanfare, however, Hewson also knew this was exactly the wrong time to be putting a period at the end of the sentence. As in any exploration at the edge of knowledge their team's sea star investigation raised as many questions, and perhaps even more, than it answered.

One new lead was particularly tantalizing. During the course of his investigations Hewson had called on Dr. Gordon Hendler, his friend and curator of echinoderms at the Los Angeles Natural History Museum. Hewson asked if he could test a few of the museum's starfish specimens that had been dated and collected decades ago. Hewson soon received 66 tissue samples of starfish that had been collected from as far back as 1915 and up to the present.

In a result that amazed Hewson and ricocheted around the whole sea star community, the SSaDV virus was found in sea stars that had been collected dating back 72 years to 1942. Haunting questions, new and old, were right back on the front burner. If this virus has been present in sea stars for 72 years, what had made it so virulent that it suddenly stripped the whole West Coast of sea stars? Was it a mutation in the virus? An environmental stressor that weakened the sea stars suddenly making them more vulnerable to the virus? And, if so which environmental stressor?

The final paragraph of the Hewson paper, far from taking a victory lap, laid out just how much there was still left to do. "However," their ending reads, "it remains to be seen how infection with SSaDV kills asteroids [sea stars], what the role is for other microbial agents associated with dying asteroids, what triggers outbreaks, and how asteroid mass mortalities will alter near-shore communities throughout the North American Pacific Coast."

For Hewson and his 25 co-authors there was no doubt what this called on them to do. It was back down the rabbit hole with science.

9

Let's Do This, Let's Get it Going
-- Dr. Joe Gaydos, DVM

SeaDoc Society, Orcas Island, Washington

Dr. Jay Gaydos, *(photo, Wendy Shattil)*

B Y 2015, A good many of the sea star questions which lent themselves to existing frameworks had been answered. Answers to the slew of remaining questions lay entangled in the complexities of the watery firmament of poorly understood oceanic forces, leaving scientists with the proverbial riddles wrapped in mysteries inside enigmas. But, as the aphorism goes on to remind, perhaps there is a key.

That year Dr. Bruce Menge and his team at Oregon State University took a renewed swing at teasing out the environmental factors that may have triggered the disease. In a massive data gathering effort along the Oregon coast, they looked at a wide range of variables from the prime suspects of ocean temperature and acidity to the seemingly trifling factors of sea star color and whether or not they resided primarily inside or outside of tide pools. Each variable was then held up against the incidence of sea star disease.

Despite the enormity of effort, when it came to ocean temperature and ocean acidity, the findings continued to be naggingly unclear with neither seeming to be a direct trigger, but with both seeming to have mediating effects. The study's more definitive results were just as vexing. The starfish residing primarily in tide pools were significantly more susceptible to disease than starfish residing mostly outside of tide pools. Additionally the purple ochre stars were significantly more vulnerable to disease than the orange stars. If somehow therein lies a key, the key itself seems exasperatingly locked in mystery.

That same year, in 2015, Seattle Aquarium along with the region's SeaDoc Society undertook an underwater dive survey of their area waters. In scores of dives by scientist divers the spectacular sunflower star was found to be "severely depleted". What they did report in a number of the afflicted areas were mushrooming populations of mussels and urchins.

At the other end of the disease range, in Ensenada, Mexico, Dr. Rodrigo Beas along with his students at Mexico's CICESE, the Ensenada Center for Scientific Research, conducted a survey of the areas coast for juvenile stars. They found exactly one - another bewildering fact, given that locations to the north were seeing an explosion of juvenile stars.

That summer Pete Raimondi and Drew Harvell teamed up with Heather Mannix of Compass, a pioneering new organization dedicated to training, connecting, and coaching scientists to communicate more effectively in public discourse on the environment. Throughout the sea star event both Raimondi and Harvell had already shown their affinity and flare for engaging with the public. Now they were preparing for a July date to brief Congress on marine diseases. They needed to make it as effective as possible. Their fervor to get it right was an early harbinger of a whole new wave of scientists polishing their communication skills and embracing opportunities to better inform public policy.

By year's end disturbing new reports of sea star wasting disease were coming in from Melbourne, Australia and from the South China Sea.

In January 2016, a little over a year after publication of Hewson's densovirus paper, Dr. Lesanna Lahner, veterinarian at Seattle Aquarium, convened a two-day sea star wasting disease summit of 30 of the scientists engaged in studying the disease. In a methodical overview the group first outlined the findings they all agreed on. They then moved on to the questions they needed to investigate, starting with listing the unanswered questions regarding the causative agent, then as regards the host, and then the environment. Lastly, they worked out future information exchanges and set standards for sampling and archiving data.

At one point in the meeting the question was asked, who has funds to continue with the work? According to Ian Hewson, he was the only one who raised his hand.

▲ ▲ ▲

But all is not groping in darkness down the oceanic rabbit hole. Technological advances enable new avenues of inquiry. For the sea star investigators the advent of real time ocean pH monitoring systems, faster genomic sequencing, and new math for analyzing mega data, are particularly welcome advances.

Dazzling as the new technology may be, it doesn't begin to match the power of the human ability to see new patterns from known facts. These patterns, in turn, guide researchers to the questions most in need of answering next.

The keystone species concept has been an obvious example in the sea star story. The understanding imparted by the keystone theory did more than just heighten initial alarm; it's now concentrating intense interest on the consequences of sea star loss to the marine ecosystem. Indeed, as predicted by the theory, in many locales hit hard by the disease there's been the expected surge in the population of mussels and urchins, the sea star's prey. Of the two, the urchins are causing the most immediate and urgent concerns.

The primary link between sea star demise and the urchin explosion is open to question. It may be due mainly to decreased predation by sea stars, as some believe, or to swarms of urchins coming out of their usual crevice habitats and taking over the vast swaths of sea floor terrain vacated by sea stars. What is grimly certain is that these unchecked plagues of spiny urchins are now literally carpeting underwater terrains and rapidly destroying huge swaths of vital kelp forests in their path.

The magnificent Pacific coast kelp forests are essential habitat, forage, and shelter for a multitude of fishes, marine mammals, sea birds, and for literally thousands of species of marine invertebrates. Most of these kelp forests have long been distressed by the hunting to near extinction of their own keystone species, the sea otter, a prolific eater of urchins. The current boost in urchin populations following the sea star losses appears to be a startling final blow to huge tracts of these kelp forests along the coast. The fear is that this may be not only a trophic cascade of the starfish intertidal ecosystem but a domino cascade of multiple marine ecosystems.

As frightening a future as these developments portend, there's a more hopeful recent concept, a new set of guiding principles, that was just gaining traction as the starfish epidemic was first taking hold. It's called One Health. It's based on a disarmingly simple understanding that the health of people, animals, and the environment are inextricably linked, and that fostering health at any point in the nexus can succeed, and perhaps can only succeed, through open, trans-disciplinary collaborations - collaborations that go beyond the usual health and wildlife scientists to include economists, educators, engineers, entomologists, hydrologists, and communities.

What at first may sound as ethereal as a new age thousand-miles-wide-and-inch-deep mantra is in reality a powerful wide angle lens that not only expands our understandings of health and disease but also most importantly promises radical new approaches to promoting planetary health.

Sea star investigators were already instinctively incorporating some of the One Health ideas into their collaborations and work. The enormous public interest in the sea star disease, in turn, has helped spread interest in the robust benefits of One Health methods and the urgency of putting them into practice.

In 2001, when Washington state's SeaDoc Society hired Joe Gaydos as their lead scientist they weren't concerned that he had virtually no experience with marine medicine. What he did have was a veterinary medical degree focused on wildlife medicine and a PhD with concentration on how disease spreads through wildlife populations. His work experience in an African wildlife park and in Central America left little doubt he could manage a leap into the sea. Nor were they put off by the fact that Gaydos wasn't much aware of the One Health concepts.

At that time One Health principles were just being pioneered by the UC Davis School of Veterinary Medicine. The school's aim was to put One Health premises into a wide range of cutting edge projects to develop and demonstrate the efficacy of the ideas.

One such project is UC Davis' Gorilla Doctors which has pulled the mountain gorillas back from near extinction in the Congo and Rwanda. This ongoing work is carried out through a wide ranging collaborative weave of local and international experts. Another of their One Health projects is PREDICT which aims to halt emerging diseases through development of social and scientific protocol sets, each tailored to the unique conditions of individual locales. And a third is EcoHealthNet which creates worldwide research networks among college and graduate students. These are just three of a dozen such innovative projects sponsored by the school.

UC Davis' SeaDoc Society was established to take the One Health concepts out to sea, in particular into the Salish Sea. As previously noted, the Salish Sea is the prolific, highly stressed body of waters encompassed by the major metropolitan areas of Seattle and Vancouver, as well as by multiple native tribes, environmental groups, and a melee of conflicting commercial interests. The immense challenges of the ecosystem are matched by a region-wide desire of its people to restore the area's incomparable marine resources, making the area fertile ground to benefit from the One Health ideas.

One of the One Health principles that has received a particularly strong boost from the sea star disease, says Gaydos, is that health and disease must be understood as a constant component of the ecosystem.

"Everybody considers such things as predation and habitat as part of the ecosystem," Gaydos explains. "Apex predators like the sea star are considered to have no natural enemies, but that's because disease is ignored." Once disease is included, he says, it's the pathogen that can be seen as the apex predator.

"Pathogens need to be monitored along with other metrics of the environment and be incorporated into restoration calculations. It's not a difficult concept once you get a chance to explain it, but it takes time to get the message out there." There's no doubt, he adds, "the sea star disease fanned those conceptual flames."

Another strand in the same line of thought provides essential counterpoint to medicine's traditional practice of one doctor treating one patient, or even one organ, in privacy. Under the One Health concepts it's the ecosystem, - the people, animals, and environment considered together - that becomes the patient. A slogan of the SeaDoc Society, in fact, is exactly that, "The entire ecosystem is our patient". Moreover, in contrast to the hermetic privacy of traditional medicine, the management of the ecosystem patient actively strives to be public and collaborative across all boundaries.

The practical implications of this One Health principle has also been brought into stark relief by the sea star demise in both a positive and negative light. On the positive side, according to all involved, it was the wide open, data sharing collaborations across countries, communities, and disciplines that so quickly yielded the wealth of findings regarding the disease. On the negative side, the spread of the sea star epidemic shows the limits of boundaries of any kind. The incapacity of marine protected areas to stave off, or even moderate, the devastation of the sea star disease has been a sobering case in point.

"When people first started talking about marine protected areas," says Gaydos, "they were often seen as a panacea, like all we have to do is set aside some areas and protect them. But the fact is that sea stars within the marine protected areas were just as afflicted as the other ones. What we're realizing over time is that marine protected areas are just one tool that we can use but they're not going to solve every problem. We're connected, like it or not, we're all connected."

Gaydos also points out the importance of keeping in mind that disease in nature isn't necessarily an environmental peril. Disease can as well be a benefit to biodiversity by knocking down the numbers in an overpopulated species and opening up niches for others. In fact, like a number of other investigators, Gaydos still hasn't ruled out the possibility that overpopulation of certain sea star species may have factored into the epidemic. He notes, as have others, that the sea stars most afflicted by the disease, the sunflower and ochre sea stars, were both extremely densely populated prior to disease outbreaks. He also laments the fact that sea stars don't form fossils making it exceptionally difficult to look back in time for clues as to whether or not this kind of epidemic has previously cycled through sea stars.

Then again, given the scope and devastation of this sea star event, in seeming rejoinder to his own thoughts he says, "A pathogen doesn't wipe out its host without a push from the environment."

At this closing juncture if you're feeling daunted, even disappointed, at the dizzying complexities at the edge of the unknowns, it's unlikely a help to say that it's always been thus. There is, however, after all, a singular, unambiguous key to any riddle wrapped in mysteries inside enigmas. It's been there, in fact, right along at every difficult turn in this star crossed story.

When the sea star disease first began erupting along the coast, says Gaydos, the email lists and social networks among the scientists "were lit on fire". Everyone knew there were likely no funds earmarked for such events, no CDC protocols to guide the path, nor any lineup of first responders. There was only a mute, mindless invertebrate in the throes of very serious trouble. But there from the beginning, to stoke the monumental efforts of monitoring, bridging disciplines, organizing citizens, brainstorming, sequencing viruses, engaging safe labs, assaying tissues, was an amazingly simple decision. As Gaydos tells it, "We all just said, 'Let's do this, let's get it going!'" And therein lies the key.

▲ ▲ ▲

When Alice found herself at the bottom of the rabbit hole, she came across a bottle that beckoned with the words "Drink Me" on its label. After much trepidation and due consideration, Alice drank her fill, and the world of wonders unfolded before her.

Acknowledgements

I'M EVER SO grateful to the marine scientists who dropped all they were doing to give generously of their time and thoughts. Some are profiled in this book. Many others, in particular Dr. Rodrigo Beas at CICESE, Ensenada, Mexico, Dr. Andrew Gunther at the Center for Ecosystem Management and Restoration, Dr. Jeff Marliave, retired chief scientist of Vancouver Aquarium, Dr. Carol Blanchette at UC Santa Barbara, Dr. Sarah Kolesar at Oregon Sea Grant, and Heather Mannix at Compass Online, gave invaluable background to the science and events.

For me, as for many, writing is at times an alluring adventure. At too many other times it's more like the old Sicilian saying, "hard bread and a knife that won't cut". So it's my great fortune to have some dynamite friends who were willing at every step to give comments, suggestions, and encouragement informed by their lifetimes of copious reading. This story simply would not have been told without them. They are Susan Moore, Roger and Kay Slagle, and Alison Edwards. Credit and thanks also goes to Kay Slagle for the cover author photo.

And a most special thanks to three professionals who took time out of their retirements to lend their expertise to the project. Dr. Jeff Marliave, retired chief scientist of Vancouver Aquarium, looked over the manuscript for general accuracy. Retired McGraw Hill editor, Barry Richman, gave generously and gently of his expert suggestions for polishing the text. And retired printer extraordinaire, George Zastrow, worked his magic with the photos.

www.ingramcontent.com/pod-product-compliance
Lightning Source LLC
Chambersburg PA
CBHW021138260726
48656CB00023B/656